SPACE

The Prophetic Frontier

Michael A. Danforth

SPACE
The Prophetic Frontier

Michael A. Danforth
Mountain Top International
PO Box 43
Yakima, Washington 98907
www.mticenter.com

All news quotes and information were copied by permission from online public resources. All the contents noted can be googled or researched as described on each page.

ISBN 0-9815944-3-3
September 2010
Printed in the United States of America

Publishing Coordinator – Ginny Seymour, publisher of Evensong Books, owner of Evensong Publishing.

Cover Graphic Designer - Tammy Dickson

He counts the number of the stars; He gives names to all of them. Great is our Lord and abundant in strength; His understanding is infinite.

Psalms 147:4-5

A CLOUD OF WITNESSES

When you live with someone like Michael it's easy to lose track of the amazing prophecies that are spoken over the years. While reading his manuscript I was surprised by all the prophetic signs and wonders that have occurred in the heavens over the last 10 years. I believe Michael's extraordinary hunger for the presence of God, at whatever the cost, plays a key role in opening up the heavenly realm to him. He is truly a man after God's own heart. The prophetic gift in him is highly contagious to anyone who longs to see into the future. **Lori Danforth (Lolly Pop) - Yakima, WA.**

Michael Danforth is one whom the "finger of God" is upon. He is a man of honor, valor and true Godly character. He is known as a pure prophetic voice with a creative cutting edge anointing. A voice God has prepared for this time and for this generation. Everything Michael does is birthed out of a deep place of intimacy with God and his secure identity as a son. His ability to flow and move in the power of the Holy Spirit is extremely refreshing and anointed. He is a gifted communicator and a true Father in the body of Christ. His heart of compassion, mercy and love marks him as the

"Real Deal". He is one whom God is using to usher in the "new wine and new wine skin". It is an honor to know him, and to call him friend. **Paula Benne- Los Angeles, CA.**

We are so thankful Michael has written this book. We were there when most of these prophecies were given, and felt the impact of the presence of God. Michael is truly tuned in to the sound of heaven and is faithful to teach us to come up higher. Seeing all these prophecies gathered together underscores their importance. God is actually shouting at us to pay attention! We don't want to be a forgetful hearer and lose the impact of His words. We want to see what our Father is doing and "engage!" **Michael and Melanie Murphy - Yakima, WA.**

Michael is a prophet of God on fire with cosmic insight! From my personal experience I find that Michael carries a great accuracy with his prophetic words. What I appreciate most about him as a person is that he is an approachable and likeable guy who has a genuine love for God and a genuine love for people. **Ginny Seymour - Lewiston, ID**

Eleven years should be sufficient time to evaluate the prophetic accuracy of someone, don't you think? Well rest assured, Michael A. Danforth has proven his connection to Holy Spirit over and over again through the fulfilled prophetic utterances he has spoken. How do I know? Because I was there for most of what is recorded in this book. And for what I have experienced myself. Read on and be encouraged. **Sharlyn Schimmels St.Hilaire - Yakima, WA.**

Jesus said of John the Baptist in Luke 7:26: "*...What did you go out to see? A prophet? Yes and I say to you much more than a prophet.*" We have known Michael Danforth for 15 years, and have had him speak at our conferences several times. Michael is much more than a prophet. He is a voice that clears the way into the Kingdom of Heaven today. He is pioneering a new breed of prophetic voices that are speaking from the heavens into the earth with a creative utterance, releasing a present Kingdom proclamation which is establishing God's will in this land. His prophetic insight of Heaven invading the earth compels the Church to arise into her heavenly position. **Mike & Ruth - Lightfoot, Nampa ID**

Michael Danforth moves so easily in the prophetic that it comes forth in every part of His ministry. He is always on the cutting edge of prophetic moves of God. Michael expresses the heart of God in a bold declaration. It is always exciting to see and hear the words that come forth and then be on the end of the fulfillment, which we have been a part of both ends of the spectrum. He is a man after God's own heart. **Gary & Sheryl - Jones Yakima, WA**

Michael is a man who lives, moves and has his being centered in the Lord. I have participated in worship with Michael for over 10 years. When Michael is “in the prophetic zone” he represents, without a doubt the heart of the Lord. I know no one more sold out to the pursuit of the kingdom of God than Michael. When he prophesies you can expect it to be headline news somewhere in the earth. He is my dearest of friends, a dedicated mentor, and one of the purest forms of Gods heart I have ever known. Michael is a treasure, destined for the nations, which God has hidden away in Yakima, Washington for a time such as this. **Steve Weise – Cowiche, WA**

Contents

Dedication

One of the primary reasons for writing this particular book was to not only honor Jesus Christ, the Lord of my life, but to honor those who have labored with me, in the Spirit. This book is a national tribute to all of my faithful friends/family who have run the race of faith with Lori and me for all of these years. Your faithful fruits of perseverance and endurance have given me strength and comfort during the most intense hours of my life. Your participation in creating an atmosphere for prophetic declarations has made it possible for the nations of the world to experience a unique realm of kingdom power and authority. The recorded experiences in this book are mantled with your tears, trials and tests. They are a sign and wonder for all who read this that a glorious generation in the kingdom of God is now at hand. You represent a generation that has given themselves to the process of heaven on earth and are now ready to become visible for all to see.

You are my dearest friends and I will always carry the deepest gratitude in my heart for the love you have shown to Lori and me throughout the years. I am so thankful that God has joined us together for such a time as this. It is my hope that we will, together, witness one of the greatest displays of the love, power, and glory of heaven the world has ever seen.

Introduction

I am someone who believes most things do not need a long introduction. I could tell you all the reasons why I felt motivated to write this book, but when you read it you will know why. I could share some intense facets of my life and the struggles I endured to get to where I am today, but when you read this book you will discover these challenges as well. In fact, there really isn't anything I could tell you to prepare you for the contents of this book. This entire edition is an introduction to knowing how to live supernaturally with the entire universe. Having said that, I need to tell you, in light of all the wonderful things I am going to share with you I have yet to discover anything greater than being in the presence of my Father. His fragrance is the Holy Chanel Number 5. Oh yes! Grace, grace, grace! Every day I am awakened by the reality of needing more and more grace in life.

In the book of Hebrews it reads:

"Therefore, since we are receiving a kingdom which cannot be shaken, let us have grace, by which we may serve God acceptably with reverence and godly fear. For our God is a

consuming fire." (Heb 12:28-29)

An unshakeable kingdom requires a whole lot of grace. This grace is the only means by which our service unto Him is deemed acceptable. We need this kind of supernatural grace because our God is a consuming fire. Many would consider it great wisdom to steer away from such a fiery blaze, while me on the other hand long to be consumed by the intensity of its flames. No one in their other mind would ever hope for such an end, but a renewed mind will settle for nothing less.

I believe everyone is challenged to find the center pulse of life. We are motivated to express the heart and mind of God that resides in us. We all have our octave, the range of the spirit that enables us to reach for the stars. I believe we are all destined to introduce something unique, divine, and everlasting into this world. You need to know that I have no desire to shine without you. I used to, but not anymore. I have no desire to go where no one has ever gone before, alone. I'm not foolish enough to actually believe others have not experienced, in some way, what I have written on the pages of this book. Though it presently seems only a minority would hope so grand, a time will come when countless other will do the same.

For the past 15 years I have asked the Lord to delay His final appearing, though I know it is still a ways down the road. Time and time again I have asked Him to extend the years of my life. I wish I would have come around much sooner in life, not wasting so many years, but no matter, I have an "in" with the giver of all life. I have discovered realms of the spirit where the very molecules of my being are altered in a single moment of heavenly exposure. He has increased the years of my life for such a time as this. I'm certainly not implying I am an old man; it's just that He has delivered me from the grip of death many times. Therefore, the life that I now live in Christ is a mere introduction to a kingdom of glory that is flooding the earth. Space is not the final frontier, but the beginning of a fresh new territory destined to reveal the knowledge and glory of God. It's one of the greatest movie screens ever created specifically designed to show the world the many mysteries of heaven. It's God's space, His frontier.

BEGINNING A NEW LIFE

"Lord, please, I want to see your glory! Please Lord, I feel like I am going to die. I have to somehow touch you or experience more of you! I'm not even sure if what I am asking is right or even permissible, but I feel a deep pain in my gut. Lord, it is the same pain I felt when my friend Billy died. This is horrible. I don't know how much longer I can live, without somehow, breaking through this darkness in my soul that seems to be keeping me from seeing You more clearly. Please, Lord, deliver me from me!"

The atmosphere in the motor home suddenly changed. I knew that someone was standing behind me, but I was afraid to look, fearful that whoever it was might leave. With all these thoughts racing through my mind, I felt this presence pass over me and fall on the bed where I was kneeling.

I remember thinking of my friend Rod Davis, who moved his family to the Dominican Republic/Haiti to start a church and minister to the people scattered throughout that region. Before leaving, he told me about an experience he had while praying in the night. The angel of the Lord walked on his bed. He said he could literally see the impressions of his feet walking on his bed. Now, here I was, living out a moment similar to his, but instead of the impressions of invisible feet, the entire bed in front of me was being weighed down by some invisible force.

While still kneeling at the bed I started laughing and crying with mixed feelings of joy and fear. It felt as though I was somewhere else, though I was still kneeling beside the bed. I could hear and feel the word of the Lord—not audibly, but in me, passing through me like the wind. I felt like an empty cup that had suddenly been filled with a surpassing knowledge of heaven. All the heaviness and darkness I was feeling in my soul just moments before was completely gone. Love—true love—had been so foreign to me, until now.

All my encounters with the Lord before this day grew dim in the light of this one glorious moment, in which I was changed into another man. A fresh new door to the kingdom of God had been opened to me. I felt like the scarecrow from the movie *The Wizard of Oz* when he discovered he had a brain. He always had a brain, he just didn't know it. This fresh knowledge of the Spirit had always been in me, I just didn't know it.

I knew the Lord had come to lie down with me that night; just like He lay down with David in green pastures and restored his soul, He restored me. The Lord kissed me that night with an everlasting love, and when He did, I awoke into a fresh new realm of spiritual understanding. Now, more than ever, I had to tell the people in my city, in the world, how wonderful He is.

A PROPHET'S INITIATION

I looked at my daughter, who was barely nine years old, and said, "Come on, Amber, let's go downtown to the back alleys and see who we can find to pray for."

She just gave me that willing smile, as if to say, "I'm with you, Dad."

So off we went, praying for drug addicts, prostitutes, runaways…anyone who would let us. We often found them standing or sitting along the building walls that outlined the alley ways of North First Street in downtown Yakima, Washington.

"Please don't let her touch me! She shouldn't be here! This is not a place for the innocent!"

Amber's tender hands caused them to respond in such a manner. Others responded with mixed feelings of conviction and comfort as her hand rested on their shoulders, asking God to heal them and bless them with His amazing love. And He did, again and again.

That was more than twenty years ago. I was fearless, bold, and full of courage, coupled with a great desire to see God's people set free. No one had to coach me to go pray for the sick. I didn't need to be convinced by some anointed ministry to go out and set the captive free. I knew what it was to be forgiven, so I was extremely motivated to see others experience the same feeling and freedom. I loved Him more than anything else in the world.

During the 1980s, although I had a prophetic edge, I was primarily doing the work of an evangelist. One day everything changed. Something in my heart changed. I was no longer compelled to do what I was doing. While I was wrestling with this change of heart, the Lord spoke these words to me:

"Do not call to mind the former things, or ponder things of the past. Behold, I will do something new, now it will spring forth; will you not be aware of it? I will even make a roadway in the

wilderness, rivers in the desert." (Isa 43:19)

I remember thinking, God, I hope so. I hope I will know it. I hope I will be aware of it when I see it.

After going through a time of feeling completely disconnected, I met an elderly man named Allen Higgins, an apostle of the Lord. He helped me identify the obvious prophetic traits that were unfolding in my life. He was the first person to really home in on the prophetic mantle that had been upon me.

Years later, in the early 1990s, I was invited by another friend to meet a prophet in Bellingham, Washington. After driving the distance, he said he didn't have time to meet with us because he had just arrived home from being out of the country. When my friend mentioned my name, the prophet said, "Wait, I do have a word for him." He told me that God had placed a strong prophetic mantle on my life and that He would confirm His word again.

After that brief prophetic encounter, we all went to a nearby coffee shop. My two friends excused themselves to use the men's room. As soon as they walked away, I had an open vision. Now if you have ever wondered whether you have had an open vision or not, most likely you haven't. When it happens, there is no doubt that you are encountering something way beyond a mental or heartfelt experience. As I sat in that crowded room of caffeinated energy, a man suddenly appeared in front of me, just a few feet away, dressed in a long hooded mantle. He walked slowly toward the exit, using the wooden staff in his hand. He did not look at me, and I couldn't see his face because of the hooded garment draped over his head. He looked like some character straight out of an ancient biblical story. Just as quickly as he appeared, he disappeared. I sat frozen, completely in awe at what I had just seen. *Was it real?*

I knew it was.

When my two friends returned, I wanted to tell them what had happened, but I wasn't even sure myself, so I kept silent. As hard as it was, I pushed the experience aside and continued with our conversation. Yet, I could not stop thinking about it. Later, as we headed south on Interstate 5, I shared my vision with my driving companion. No sooner had I finished describing what I had encountered when the same ancient man appeared in front of us, crossing the highway.

I screamed out, “There he is! There he is again! Can you see him?”

My friend laughed with amazement. “No, but I feel an unusual presence of the Lord in the car with us right now.”
Although we were moving along at 65 mph plus, the distance between us and this mysterious man never changed. Once again, I could not see the man’s face, but this time he spoke. “The scepter is in the high place.” Then he was gone.

At that moment I saw a golden scepter lying against a very large rock at the top of a steep mountain on the other side of the road in front of us. As I looked at this glorious treasure, I knew it wasn’t just an object to be had, but it was a realm in the spirit I was destined to enter into. Just as the vision started to blur away, the brilliance of the scepter illuminated 100 times over, branding my heart and mind with an intense desire to find that place in God.

Little did I know I was destined to see this ancient character one last time. A couple of months later, a group of us were praying in a mansion in Yakima, Washington. My wife and I were caretakers of the property at the time. As we prayed, I suddenly became caught up in a vision, not an open vision

like before, but in the spirit of my mind I could see this ancient man, mantled with the same hooded coat, staff in hand, moving along ever so slowly just as before. This time I started running after him, desperately wanting to see who he was. I ran with all my might, but I could barely keep up with him, even though he was moving very slowly. In the next moment, I was shoulder to shoulder with him, leaning forward like a runner trying to cross the finish line before anyone else. As I leaned past the edge of the hooded mantle covering his head, I looked up into his eyes and screamed, “Oh my God! It’s me! The ancient man is me!”
I looked around the room at the startled faces, shocked at my sudden outburst.
“It’s me!” I cried. “I looked into his eyes and saw myself!”

The others simply stared at me, stunned, trying to process what I had just said.

“I know this sounds crazy, but I saw myself in another time—in the future.” I explained what I had seen. “When I looked into his eyes, I saw myself. He didn’t look like me, but his eyes were my eyes. I recognized his movements as those of the Spirit of the Lord. I was running with all my might and he was barely moving along. He moved seemingly without any effort and was still able to move faster than me, even though I was running harder than I could possibly run. In that moment an unusual realm of wisdom and understanding came over me.

"I knew I wasn't seeing an angel, but a man in the future who had given himself totally over to the Spirit of God" I paused briefly, catching my breath.

"I realized this man wasn't just a reflection of me in the future, he represented a future generation that would go to the high places of the Spirit and lay hold of the scepter of God. They will buy gold refined in the fire and move supernaturally throughout the earth."

Overwhelmed by the powerful emotion of my experience, I looked around the room and saw the others with me were also deeply moved by what had just happened. Then we burst out into laughter—a laughter generated by an unusual presence and glory of the Lord. This was my initiation into the prophet's mantle.
I have since learned that God will most always initiate your spiritual transition through some divine encounter. For Noah it was an ark. For Abraham it was a covenant experience coupled with a vision of future generations as numerous as the stars. For

Moses it was a burning bush, and for David it was the word of a prophet named Samuel that changed the course of his life forever. I have long remembered those words: **"The scepter is in the high place."** A short time later, Mountain Top International was born.

SPACE: THE PROPHETIC FRONTIER

From that moment on I began to see and hear differently. I later realized that by looking into the eyes of this ancient one, I had received new sight. I was now seeing the present from the perspective of the future, stronger than ever before. It was then when the Lord revealed to me how some people evolve from one function to the next.

Previously in my life, I had been functioning primarily as a prophetic evangelist, then a prophet. I know the time will come when I will fully enter into the realm of a seer. I am referring to a seer as someone who is influenced by the power of the Holy Spirit to see into the invisible realm and the future intentions of God. I have since had various experiences that pertain to this particular function in the spirit in a profound way. I am a firm believer that God has given everyone the power of sight—beyond present-day circumstances. It's just a matter of being exposed to different realms of the Spirit, thus exercising our spiritual senses. Seeing is not just seeing beyond the present, it's seeing the invisible kingdom of heaven become visible.

During the earlier years of my ministry, I didn't focus on being a prophet as much as just wanting to be in the presence of the Lord. Everything else just seemed to fall into place. To be honest, I might have leaned a bit too far the other way. In fact, many times I tried to distance myself from both the title of "prophet" and other prophets largely due to the extreme abuses I had encountered along the way. Many people want to be a prophet, and many are self-appointed.

I have since learned that someone else's spiritual abuses or exaggerations do not have to become mine. The most important thing is to be you. Find out who you are in God and be that person in the kingdom of God.

These pages were born out of a 12 year process of hearing God speak to me about unusual discoveries and movements in space, and the heavens above. I know, for some readers, the experiences I'm going to share will sound a bit outrageous. Yet everything written has publicly been witnessed as it occurred and was archived in written or audio format. The fulfillment of every prophetic occurrence outlined in this book has been announced by national media one way or another. If you would like to investigate the details of these events more thoroughly, I encourage you to Google the media titles provided throughout this book. Most of these words and their fulfillment can also be viewed on our website at www.mticenter.com.

Some have labeled me a "prophet of the cosmos," but I simply see myself as being in a season in which God has chosen to reveal various movements in the outer limits as a prophetic wonder and sign of His kingdom increasing in earth. The things He has shown me about the future are by no means confined to the outer limits. Some pertain to the skies above which also has a spiritual significance in the earth. According to the Bible, **all** of creation reveals the attributes of God's glory.

"For since the creation of the world His invisible attributes, His eternal power and divine nature, have been clearly seen, being understood through what has been made, so that they are without

excuse." (Romans 1:20)

My earliest recollection of encountering the prophetic frontier of space was after we moved the ministry of Mountain Top International to Fruitvale Avenue in Yakima, Washington. A group of us gathered early in the morning two or three days each week to worship the Lord. Our morning gatherings became a centerpiece for God to reveal to me—to us—some amazing movements on earth and the increase of His kingdom.

I remember the time when it really hit me that God was showing me certain movements in space. Honestly, it seemed a bit maddening to me. It was already a challenge for the people in our city to accept the idea that a prophet was living in their midst, let alone hear that we were prophesying about unusual activity in space—much of which had not yet come to pass. Most of what I receive from the Spirit comes primarily through the spontaneity of the spirit, specifically spontaneous worship. The phrase "spontaneous worship" can have different meanings for people. To me, "spontaneous worship" is when you play music and sing songs that are unrehearsed. This means you do not know what key you are going to play in or what lyrics you are going to sing until you start playing and singing in the moment. Worship has always played an important role for me in hearing the Lord's voice and seeing into the future—not that I can't hear or see otherwise, but it certainly opens up a unique realm for me in the spirit.

It might not seem like such a big deal now, but when I started engaging in public spontaneous worship in 1998 and then more frequently in 2000, to most people in our area, it was a bit outrageous—even cultish to some. They questioned how we were supposed to worship God if we don't have the lyrics to the songs. Ha! It sounds humorous now, but then it was a major roadblock for those who were of less prophetic persuasion. Interestingly enough, because of that little bit of difference, for a long time we were considered outcasts.

So I'm sure you can appreciate my reasoning for feeling like the whole cosmos thing was a bit maddening as well. All we needed was one more log to throw onto the fire of an already burning rejection toward Mountain Top International.

Madness or not, we couldn't help but press onward into another inviting realm of the Spirit of God, regardless of the consequences. In 2002 the Lord started speaking to me about keeping a consistent diary—an archive of our worship gatherings and prophetic declarations. Prior to that time, many prophetic words that were spoken during our worship gatherings about many things—including the outer limits of space—were not archived. Thus, even though I have some recollection of those times, I have chosen to share only the times that are vivid in my memory and the ones we have recorded.

INSPIRE THE UNIVERSE

God has given us the power to create movement in the heavens above and earth below. He has given us the power to inspire the universe. There are no limits as to how far the spoken word of God can reach. Every praise and worship inspired by the Lord is destined to change the world and encourage the work of His hands. Just as the writers of the gospel were inspired by the Holy Spirit to articulate the works of Jesus and the intentions of the Father's heart, we too are equally inspired as Jesus was to become the voice of our Father, signifying our heavenly origin. As a prophetic psalmist, David revealed this particular sphere of understanding.

"Praise the LORD! Praise the LORD from the heavens; Praise Him in the heights! Praise Him,

all His angels; Praise Him, all His hosts! Praise Him, sun and moon; Praise Him, all stars of light! Praise Him, highest heavens, and the waters that are above the heavens! Praise the LORD from the earth, Sea monsters and all deeps; Fire and hail, snow and clouds; Stormy wind, fulfilling His word; mountains and all hills; Fruit trees and all cedars; beasts and all cattle; creeping things and winged fowl; kings of the earth and all peoples; princes and all judges of the earth; both young men and virgins; old men and children." (Psalms 148:1-4, 7-12)

I find these scriptures absolutely astonishing. David is encouraging all of creation to praise the Lord. How can this be? Other than mankind, creation is not self-conscious. It's not like the sun and moon are contemplating fizzling out and, as such, need to be encouraged to continue shining. Yet this is in fact what David is encouraging, telling the sun, moon, and stars to shine and praise their creator. Undoubtedly these praises from David had an impact on creation. Indeed, this is what creation has always longed for: for the sons of God to exercise their true kingdom state in the earth.

When God created the first man and placed him in

a garden of endless beauty, He told him to tend and keep it **(Gen 2:15).** Much of our conception of a garden is one that requires some watering and a whole lot of weeding, but I assure you, this was not the kind of tending and keeping that was needed in the Genesis era. The toiling of today did not come into play until after the initial act of disobedience **(Gen 3:18-19).** I believe the caring of Eden initially came through the sound of a man's words, his presence, and the touch of his hands—the same type of care that man received from the Lord while living in a land of perfect peace.

"And they heard the sound of the LORD God walking in the garden in the cool of the day...." (Gen 3:8)

In the beginning, mankind was inspired by the sound of the Lord. They were encouraged by His words and the touch of His presence and glory. They were moved by creation around them. This is still the case today. Every created thing is deeply touched by His presence and motivated by His words. When David worshipped and sang his praises, his words and sounds released a powerful force of heaven unto the earth. David was exercising his kingdom authority. The praises of David had the ability to inspire all of creation to praise the Lord. He inspired the heavens, the angels, the sun and the moon, the stars, and the waters in the heavens above. This is amazing! David knew what it was like to have true spiritual dominion in the earth.

When was the last time you worshipped the Lord and—during that time—inspired all of creation to fulfill their ordained purpose in life? This is a wonderful insight into having global dominion wherever you go and one of the keys to having dominion over much of the negative impact that tries to create havoc on earth. Although we are surrounded by all kinds of opposing forces—both natural and spiritual—the resources that are available to us are without measure.

When Jesus and the disciples were in a boat crossing from one shore to another, a great storm arose. During the storm, Jesus was asleep. As the storm became increasingly violent, the disciples—fearing for their lives—woke Jesus. Jesus responded in this manner:

"And He got up and rebuked the wind and said to the sea, "Hush, be still." And the wind died down and it became perfectly calm. And He said to them, "Why are you afraid? Do you still have no

faith?" They became very much afraid and said to one another, "Who then is this, that even the wind and the sea obey Him?" (Mark 4:39-41)

Now let's put this into perspective. They're in a storm, on a boat, and Jesus rebukes the wind and commands the sea to be still. This storm was most likely the result of what causes every other storm at sea: natural high and low atmospheric pressures at work. Yet, regardless of its cause, Jesus still had the authority to interrupt the forces of nature, bringing them into submission to His will. Creation does not have a will of its own. It does not govern itself. It's governed by the word of the Lord. Its very existence was put in place by God.

I understand that today's natural conditions are much different than they were prior to flooding in the days of Noah. The weather is different, the planet is different, the world is different, but try telling that to Jesus. None of that mattered to Him. When Jesus decided to intervene and command the wind and waters to be still, they had no choice but to obey. Jesus is our ultimate example of authority and power. Before Jesus departed, he left us with this amazing reality:

"Truly, truly, I say to you, he who believes in Me, the works that I do, he will do also; and greater *works* than these he will do; because I go to the Father. Whatever you ask in My name, that will I do, so that the Father may be glorified in the Son. If you ask Me anything in My name, I will do *it.*" (John 14:12-14)

Wow! How cool is that! This is not a time to say "it's not working!" Instead, it is time to keep on declaring, keep on prophesying the word of the Lord, knowing that the heavens above and earth below will move according to the love and power of God working within us.

I want to remind you of the words of Elisha. After commanding the water to fill the ditches of the king, Elisha said, **"This is but a slight thing (an easy thing) in the sight of the LORD; He will also give the Moabites into your hand" (2Kings 3:18).** King Hezekiah was near death, and Isaiah came to him and told him to get his affairs in order because he was going to die. After hearing this, Hezekiah cried out to the Lord to let him live. The Lord heard the cry and before Isaiah could get past the inner court of the palace, told Isaiah to go back and retract his words **(2Kings 20:1-4).**

"Return and say to Hezekiah the leader of My people, 'Thus says the LORD, the God of your father David, "I have heard your prayer, I have seen your tears; behold, I will heal you. On the third day you shall go up to the house of the LORD." (2Kings 20:5)

Through the prophet Isaiah, God increased the years of Hezekiah by fifteen years **(2Kings 20:6).** Isaiah then gave instructions to Hezekiah in order for his healing to be complete. However, Hezekiah wanted a sign from God that he would, in fact, be healed. Can you blame the guy? Imagine the emotional rollercoaster he must have been on. One minute you're told to pack your bags, you're going to die; then, while your face is still wet with tears of desperation, God decides to give you fifteen more years. That would make anyone a nervous wreck! No wonder Hezekiah asked for some kind of confirmation that everything was really going to happen. Here we can read how Isaiah gave Hezekiah the option of seeing the shadow of the sun go forward or backwards:

"Isaiah said, "This shall be the sign to you from the LORD, that the LORD will do the thing that He has spoken: shall the shadow go forward ten steps

or go back ten steps?" So Hezekiah answered, "It is easy for the shadow to decline ten steps; no, but let the shadow turn backward ten steps." Isaiah the prophet cried to the LORD, and He brought the shadow on the stairway back ten steps by which it had gone down on the stairway of Ahaz." (2Kings 20:9-11)

Now, scientifically I'm not sure how all that works. Either the earth changes its rotation or the shadow moves out of sync with the sun. Either way, it's pretty darned impressive. I think most of us know what it is like to face circumstances that look impossible to overcome. We need the mindset of Elisha and Isaiah. We need the kind of faith and confidence in God that expects creation to enforce the word of the Lord. We should be able to look at any opposing circumstance in our life and declare, "This is an easy thing in the eyes of the Lord." It's time we look at the current condition of our nation and declare, "This is a very simple thing for God to fix." The entire universe is postured to move at our command. All of creation is ready to respond to the faith of God working within us. We have shifted into another realm of kingdom authority like no other generation before us. Come on!

Like David, we can speak to the sun and moon and say, "Give praises to your creator! Shine like you have never shined before! Come on, stars, be brilliant today! Let the people know that your creator is the master of the universe!" How outrageous is that? If we can see the encouraging influence that God has given to us, we can impact the world in unimaginable ways.

I recently shared a prophetic word with a friend about his ability to inspire creation with the sound that God had given to him. I said,

"Randy, every time I see you, I see this incredible realm of influence you have in your life to inspire the creation of God supernaturally. I believe the sound of heaven in you has the power to literally captivate every creature in the earth."

His eyes widened with excitement and he said, "Michael, not too long ago my wife, Tammy, and I were sitting out on our porch. While I was playing my guitar, a Mountain Bluebird came and landed on the head of my instrument. As I continued to play, Tammy and I both stared in absolute amazement. The bird just sat there, as if it were being captivated by what was being played."

As Randy continued to share his amazing story, I began to see how all of creation was eager to respond to the glorious manifestation of God's people on earth.

In Psalms, David gives us more supernatural insight as to the nature of our dominion on earth.

"When I consider Your heavens, the work of Your fingers, The moon and the stars, which You have ordained; What is man that You take thought of him, And the son of man that You care for him? Yet You have made him a little lower than God, And You crown him with glory and majesty! You make him to rule over the works of Your hands; You have put all things under his feet..."(Ps 8:3-6)

David was so overwhelmed by the enormous reality of the cosmos that it caused him to wonder how God could have ever been mindful of mankind in light of the splendor above. He raised the question as to why God would even take the time to make Himself known to the son of man in light of His universal handiwork. David expressed that the order of man is just a little lower than God. What a wonderful picture of what it means to be created in the image and likeness of God! Such mindfulness is crowned with glory and honor. David's final summary of man in this particular passage concluded with the dominion that God has given to us over the works of His hands. Wow! What a glorious revelation of God's true intentions toward us! It's no wonder the earth groans for the full awakening of the body of Christ. All of creation is eager to respond to the sound of heaven within us.

In the near future, we will surely start witnessing extraordinary activities amongst creation. This is more than the simple appreciation of seeing the beauty and hearing the sounds while strolling through the park. I'm talking about the kind of activity where nature itself begins to respond to the Spirit of God working in us in unimaginable ways. This is truly a **Narnia** moment. Creation is literally beginning to move to the rhythm of eternity currently flowing out of our bellies. This eternal realm of the spirit is causing the creativity within us to take on a form that emphatically emanates the nature of God on earth.

While driving to a meeting at the Healing Rooms in Spokane, Washington, I saw an extremely large and bright rainbow in the sky. From my viewpoint, the rainbow appeared to be vertical, like the colored spectrum of bars on an old television set. Then something unusual caught my eye. The single barred rainbow was so bright that it began to reflect itself many times over. Now I have seen a double rainbow and even a quadruple rainbow, but until that time I had never seen an octuple rainbow: At least eight single bars were reflecting all the spectrums of a normal rainbow, with the center rainbow being the most evident. In that moment, I had a revelation of how the brightness of the Lord was being multiplied many times over because of His radiant glory. The apostle Paul described it like this:

"But we all, with unveiled face, beholding as in a mirror the glory of the Lord, are being transformed into the same image from glory to glory, just as from the Lord, the Spirit." (2Cor 3:18)

The multiplicity of this radiant glory within both you and me is stirring the entire universe. The mysteries in the heavens above are making a divine entrance for all to see. The hour of global discovery is upon us.

HIDDEN IN PLAIN SIGHT

In keeping with a universal perspective, we are beginning to see what we could not see before. Things that were once hidden are being revealed. As my brother-in-law, Gary, once said, "Hidden in plain sight." Ha! You gotta love it! Oddly enough, Mountain Top International has been hidden in plain sight for years. We could have stood out in the middle of the road, waving a red flag, and everyone still would have passed us by. Yet there comes a time when ears and eyes are opened for the first time—opened to new realms of the Spirit, new truths, objects of creation, and the gift within us. For those of you who have felt like your ideas, your perception of life, your kingdom views and desires have been invisible to the rest of the world, let me encourage you to stay your course in God. A great awakening is rising on earth, and the glory in you is destined to be revealed. Millions will suddenly hear and see what they could not hear or see before, even though it was in plain sight the entire time.

I recently read an article from a magazine someone gave me called *Sky and Telescope*, which the magazine suggests is "the essential magazine of astronomy." I don't normally sit around and read magazines on astronomy; however, the front page of this July 2010 edition caught my eye. It read, "Hidden in Plain Sight." The featured article was about a soap bubble nebula discovered by an amateur astronomer named Dave Jurasevich. The article described this modern-day astronomer, who found a deep-sky object hiding in plain sight. Just imagine: All the greatest professional astronomers in the world had been looking over the same areas of space again and again, but it was an amateur astronomer who realized that something had been hidden right in front of them the whole time. This is a perfect analogy of the hour in which we are living.

Sometimes we can be so fixated on the complexity of life that we fail to see the obvious object right in front of us. You are that seer. You are that discoverer. You are the ones who are destined to reveal the obvious. When you see it, when you find it, your testimony will be, "It was hidden in plain sight the whole time."

I am reminded of two men in the Bible who were headed to a village called Emmaus. While they were on their journey, Jesus met up with them,

"But their eyes were prevented from recognizing Him" (Luke 34:13-32).

When Jesus spoke to them, His words were so intense that they were burned in the men's hearts. Still unaware that they were talking to Jesus, they pleaded with Him to stay the night. Once they sat down and began to commune with Him, their eyes were opened. Imagine how they must have felt when they realized that the very topic of their previous road trip had been right in front of them the whole time. This is another example of a new season in the Spirit that we are entering into.

The eyes of countless people who were once restrained from seeing the obvious will see clearly. This new sight is being instigated by an unusual fellowship in the spirit realm. The blindness and obstructions that were previously in the way are being removed. The things that were once invisible are becoming more and more visible every day.

NEW PLANETS

One of the signs of the kingdoms of this world being influenced by the kingdom of God is that the actions of world kingdoms will create spiritual sight rather than spiritual blindness. For decades, the kingdom of God has been veiled to most of the world's population. Most of the world's media has tried to filter out the truth. This situation is rapidly changing. Although gross darkness is still very evident, many of these kingdoms are being influenced by the prevailing force of heaven. Hollywood is being invaded by an invisible energy that is influencing writers, directors, and actors for the greater good. Billionaires are being motivated to pour endless resources into charities and kingdom works around the world. Science is continuing to discover new technology that affords scientists new sight into the farthest regions of space. These new technologies have been quite instrumental in confirming a variety of prophetic declarations about the cosmos.

On the morning of **February 11, 2004,** the Lord gave me this prophetic word at a Mountain Top Gathering in Yakima, WA:

"Will you look to space once again? For new planets shall appear. Planets they will say are new, but they were there all the time. And what will they say of water. Water in space! You laugh, but soon you will see new planets appear and even water in space, says the Spirit of the Lord. For this is the time for the eyes of my people to be opened like never before. They will see further than they have ever seen before and they will hear what they could not hear. So look to the sky, even to space and declare, "I can see! I can see! You can see!" Come on! Give Him praise...."

A couple of years later, various news reports of newly confirmed planets began to surface from all over the world. Since then, one finding after another has been documented. In 2010 alone, the discovery of new planets was off the charts. It's important to note that, prior to this prophetic declaration in February 2004, there had been no solid affirmations of newly discovered planets for decades. The following examples provide just a few headlines about the finding of new planets since that day in 2004.

Jan 8, 2005

LOS ANGELES — Astronomers announced Friday that they have discovered a new planet larger than Pluto in orbit around the sun, likely renewing debate over what exactly is a planet and whether Pluto should keep its status. Below is an artist's concept of such planet.

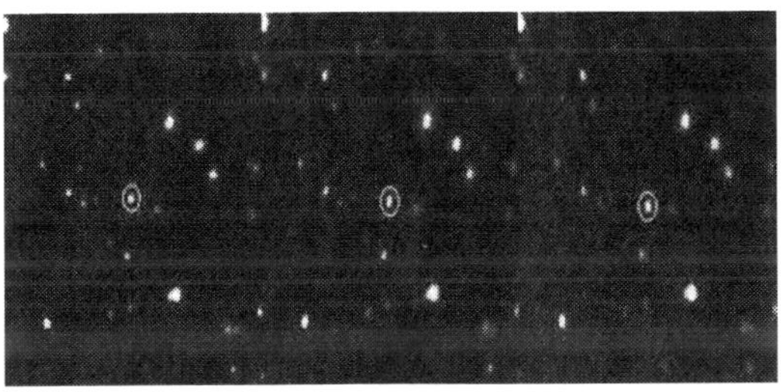

Image above: These time-lapse images of a newfound planet in our solar system, **called 2003UB313**, were taken on Oct. 21, 2003, using the Samuel Oschin Telescope at the Palomar Observatory near San Diego, Calif. The planet, circled in white, is seen moving across a field of stars. The three images were taken about 90 minutes apart. **Scientists did not discover that the object in these pictures was a planet until Jan. 8, 2005. Image credit: Samuel Oschin Telescope, Palomar Observatory.**

Additional Headlines:

“New Planet "Bonanza" Discovered at Center of Milky Way.” Blake de Pastino in Washington, DC
National Geographic News, October 4, 2006

“A "bonanza" of new planets has been found at the heart of our galaxy, NASA astronomers announced today.” “Sixteen potential planets have been detected in the region known as the Galactic Bulge, the mass of stars and hot gas at the center of the Milky Way some 26,000 light-years away.”

National Geographic News Reports: January 4, 2010

Five New Planets Found; Hotter Than Molten Lava

Seven new planets discovered!

The discovery of our universe is expanding!

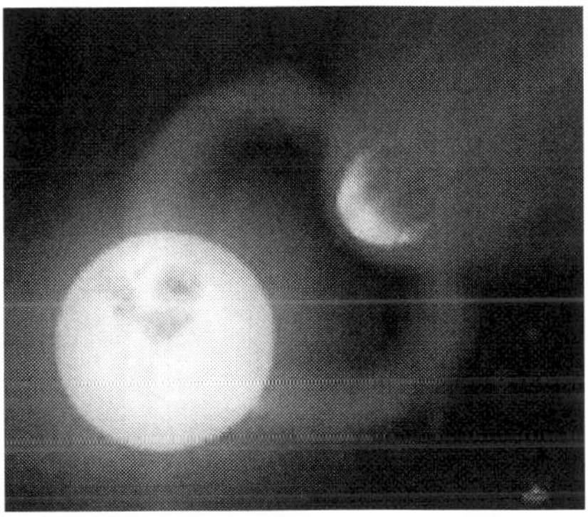

London: An international team, including scientists from the Oxford University, has discovered seven diverse new planets, from "shrunken-Saturns" to "bloated hot Jupiters", as well as a rare brown dwarf with 60 times the mass of Jupiter. (June 14, 2010)

WATER IN SPACE

The later part of this prophetic declaration was the discovery of water in space. It probably doesn't seem like such a big deal now, but before the national media made its announcement to the world, it was a very big deal. Most people would have thought it was absurd to hear one day they would fine water in space.

“NASA's Phoenix Mars Lander has confirmed the existence of water ice on Mars. Mission scientists celebrated the news after a sample of the ice was finally delivered to one of the Lander’s instruments. Phoenix's mission has also officially been extended for one month beyond its original mission, NASA announced today at a briefing at the University of Arizona at Tucson, where mission control is currently based.
"I'm very happy to announce that we've gotten an ice sample," said the University of Arizona's William Boynton, co-investigator for Phoenix's Thermal and Evolved-Gas Analyzer (TEGA), which heats up samples and analyzes the vapors they give off to determine their composition.
"We have water," Boynton added. "We've seen evidence for this water ice before in observations by the Mars Odyssey orbiter and in disappearing chunks observed by Phoenix last month, but this is the first time Martian water has been touched and tasted."

It was recently announced that the moon had more ice below its surface than previously realized.

So why would God prophetically reveal these things before they are actually discovered or realized? God loves using His own creation to announce to the world, “I am here! I am speaking to you,” thereby conveying important messages to His people and the world. In this case, God’s intent is revealed in the latter part of this prophetic word.

[Th]is is the time for the eyes of my people to be [op]ened like never before. They will see further than they have ever seen before and they will hear what they could not hear…." (portion of February 11, 2004 prophecy)

These national broadcasts were not just about the discovery of new planets or water in space; they were not simply reporting that NASA was seeing further into the cosmos. These articles were about the sight of God's people going to the next level, marking the beginning of the people of God seeing more and hearing more than any other generation. Without a doubt, another veil has been ripped away. The Spirit of God is making way for a fresh new breed of hearers and seers to rise up in the kingdom of God.

After this prophetic word came into fruition, it indeed seemed like the spirit realm and the cosmos shifted into another gear, revealing many hidden secrets. Revelation is like that.

The true meaning of this declaration, "Water in space" is seeing and discovering something that was there all the time, yet hidden in plain sight. I am of the mind that certain prophetic declarations cause movement.

Prophecy is not about just predicting the future, but creating it. For some, this is a hard truth to swallow, but those who have engaged in this kind of spiritual activity know it's a very easy thing for God to do. It's not uncommon for the word of the Lord to create movement. It's not uncommon for conditions to change around you because of prophetic declarations. Again, there's a difference between predicting movement and creating it. Prophetic predictions are based on knowledge or impressions about the future activity of man or the intentions of God toward His people. This knowledge includes various activities on earth and in the heavens.

You can also pick up something about the future based on current actions, although in my estimation this can prove to be very unreliable. Actions from both perspectives, predicting and creating, are subject to change; therefore, the outcome can differ from what was previously prophesied. Prophetic declarations have many variables in the spirit; you learn them as you go. I could write a whole different book on this particular subject, so let me get to my point. Creating the future is something much different than just predicting it. It involves a unique alignment with the heart and intentions of God in such a manner that creation literally moves in response to the spoken word of God. When this occurs, you are not just predicting an event, you are creating motion. I have always been bothered by men and women who prophecy about horrible things in the future and leave you with the feeling that there is nothing you can do about it. What's up with that? I'm glad Moses wasn't of that mind when God wanted to wipe out the entire human race—again—and start over with his prized servant Moses. When prophetic declarations break the barrier of forecasting the future, they emanate an unusual force of kingdom persuasion, placing a command on creation to respond to the sudden impulse of heaven. Yes, this is huge, but this is the future expectations for generations to come.

I have followed behind prophets and prophetesses who have given words of destruction for certain areas. Without any knowledge of what was prophesied, I have contradicted the prophetic word that was previously spoken. Does this mean they are wrong and I'm right? Not necessarily. I believe that what they were hearing and seeing was possibly very real and very much God. Nonetheless, I was being prompted by the Spirit of God to declare otherwise. It almost sounds like God is contradicting Himself, which He is not. Revealing to someone about possible destruction in the future doesn't make it automatic. Rather, it means that if you stay the current course this is what you can expect to see happen. This does not imply the initial intentions of God toward His people, which we know are good and not evil.

I know there are times when a word of prophetic discipline can be declared, but you must be very careful that your personal displeasures are not mistaken for God's displeasures. The first word spoken can be the sound of warning while the second is the sound of promise. Just because we hear and see something that is uninviting doesn't mean we can't change the outcome. I would rather err on the side of prevention rather than on the side of consenting to death and destruction. Since the beginning of time, we have been able to see where God has given humanity the power of persuasion, the power to change His mind, and the power to change the future course of events. As previously mentioned, we can see this type of action in the life of Moses. We can also read where Abraham intervened on behalf of Sodom and Gomorrah. Although both cities were still destroyed, we were given a clear picture of the willingness of God to give audience to Abraham.

God wasn't just amusing Abraham by listening to his plea for the few righteous who still remained in

Sodom; He was giving him the opportunity to weigh in on the justice at hand.

God is not without emotion. He is not without love and compassion. If that were the case, you and I would not be here today. When God spoke to Moses concerning the nation of Israel He said,

"Now, behold, the cry of the sons of Israel has come to Me; furthermore, I have seen the oppression with which the Egyptians are oppressing them." (Ex 3:9)

I believe that God is always persuaded for the greater good. He loves us and takes great joy in giving us good and wonderful things. God loves to show us the future. He enjoys revealing to us events that are scheduled to take place in earth, on earth, and above earth—yes, even in the cosmos. God created us to walk into the light, not remain in the dark and unknown. It is His delight to share with us His deepest secrets. We were created to see as He sees and to think the way He thinks.

THE MILKY WAY

On **June 15, 2005**, at one of our worship gatherings on Fruitvale Avenue in Yakima, Washington, I prophesied that the Milky Way was changing form. Now mind you, I had always imagined that the Milky Way was this huge mass of innumerable stars since the beginning of creation and would always be the same until the end of time. Like all the other words given to me by God about the cosmos, I felt a little bit disturbed by what was coming out of my mouth. I still remember some of the faces looking at me then, as if to say, "Michael has really lost it this time." These are the words that I declared that particular Wednesday morning in 2005.

"Look! Look! Look at the Milky Way for it is changing, it is moving. I don't know if it really

does move, but I hear the spirit of the Lord say, it's changing; it is moving! Why? Because it will be a sign to you that my body and this nation are beginning to change; they are taking on another form, says the Spirit of the Lord. A form unlike any you have ever seen before. Truly the latter form will be greater than the former, says the Spirit of the Lord! So see the change! See the movement! Feel the shift in the earth even now!..."

Little did we know that the revelation of that day would actually come into being within a few short years. This is always the intriguing part about prophetic words for the future. Unless a specific timeline is given, you never really know when it will come into being. However, the moment the word is released, it feels as though it is happening right then. In some ways it is, because, in the spirit, the timeline between the present and the future seems to be broken and what feels like tomorrow is really today, even though it might not reveal itself until months or years down the road.

The more you act upon this kind of prophetic impulse the more familiar you become with this particular realm of the spirit. In **January 2009,** this is was one of the many headlines printed about the

Milky Way:

"Milky Way Changes Its Mass!"
By Rachel Courtland
Space…17:04 20 January, 2009

NewScientist

"Earlier this month, astronomers announced a new measurement of the Milky Way's mass—saying it is 50% heftier than thought and about as heavy as our nearest large neighbor, Andromeda."

"The new result is a major revision and a full three times larger than another team's recent estimate. It also raises a question: why don't astronomers know how much our home galaxy weighs?"

Now, in keeping with my previous thought about predicting future movement versus creating it, this prophetic word would fall under the auspice of prediction. According to other articles about the Milky Way, it already could have been getting more dense, or it was far denser than first realized. However, the fact remains: they did not know it. It did not become a national phenomenon until after the word of the Lord was given. Once again, please note the purpose of God for revealing this event in advance. He is giving sight to His people, before the discovery, not after. According to science, the Milky Way had increased its speed to such a degree that it had become denser, thereby changing its form or mass.

So what does this mean to you and me? It means that this nation and the body of Christ are changing, taking on another form. As you read this prophetic word, it describes how our form or shape will be unlike anything we have ever seen before. It concludes that the latter form will be greater than the former. Remember, this word was spoken in 2005 and its fruition actually occurred in January 2009. For those of you who have been paying close attention to the government in this nation, you are aware that 2009 marked the beginning of a major change in our nation. Needless to say the government of today is much different than anything we have ever seen before. We are also witnessing a major transformation within the body of Christ. The platform for preaching the kingdom of God is dramatically changing and will never be the same again. Through the various venues of the media—especially the internet—the kingdom of God is expanding exponentially.

In my previous book *Evolution of Another Kind*, I spoke about the internet and how it would become the leading worldwide distributor of the kingdom of God in the future. It seems like a no-brainer now, but the book was written in 2005 and published in 2008. In that space of time, the gospel of Jesus Christ via the internet has flown off the charts. The body of Christ is currently undergoing one of the greatest transformations ever encountered since the birth of the early Christian church. Exactly how the body of Christ will appear remains to be seen, but one thing we know for certain is that the latter form will be much greater than the former.

SUPERNATURAL RAINBOWS

While I am on the subject of changing forms, I would like to share with you a couple of events directly related to the spiritual transformation moving across the globe. On **May 14, 2006,** during a conference at Mountain Top International in Yakima, Washington, I prophesied about an unusual form of the rainbow that would be displayed in the skies. The following text highlights the rainbow word.

"Watch the rainbow! For it is beginning to change! Its very form is changing now. You will see colors of the rainbow you have never seen before. This will be a sign to you that My promises are altering the form of My people in the earth right now, and you will see them in a light and glory you have never seen them in before."

I like how the Lord said, **"This will be a sign to you that My promises are altering the form of My people in the earth right now, and you will see them in a light and glory you have never seen them in before."**

Now take a look at the national publication of this prophetic fulfillment. NATIONAL GEOGRAPHIC

Photo in the News: Rare "Rainbow" Spotted Over Idaho

Report on June 19, 2006— "It looks like a rainbow that's been set on fire, but this phenomenon is as cold as ice. Known in the weather world as a circum-horizontal arc, this rare sight was caught on film on June 3 as it hung over northern Idaho near the Washington State border. This particular arc spanned several hundred square miles of sky and lasted for about an hour, according to the **London *Daily Mail.***

This rainbow event could have occurred anywhere in the United States or even the world, but it happened on the border between Washington and Idaho. This prophetic word implies the people who are taking God at His word are being transformed into a glorious display of His love and power unlike any other time.

I remember this word well because after posting it on the internet, we received numerous reports via email from people all over the Northwest who had witnessed unusual rainbow forms. As you can see, this event became a national phenomenon before settling back down to its usual field of display.

It never ceases to amaze me how God uses the beautiful works of His hands to paint a picture of hope and promise across the skies for all to see. I know that many of you have been waiting for God's promises to be fulfilled in your life. Be assured that God is currently using all of creation as a divine canvas to illustrate His love toward you. He is letting you know that He hasn't forgotten you and that all of His promises toward you are destined to be fulfilled in your lifetime. We truly do have a wonderful Father—a Father who loves us and watches over us, a Father who colors our world with everlasting hope.

GLORIOUS BIG DIPPER

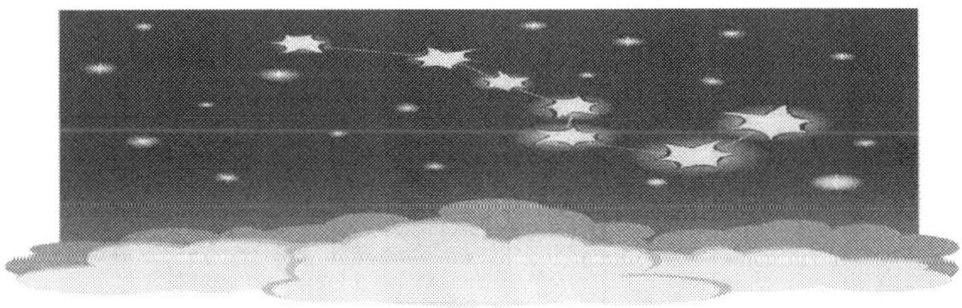

In 2009, I spoke at a gathering at Mountain Top International, then at a conference in Manson, Washington, a neighboring city to Chelan, and again in Spokane, Washington. At these meetings, I shared a prophetic word the Lord had given to me about the changing formations of the stars. I shared this same word again, but in more detail, on one of our radio programs, "Danforthlive," which you can also listen to online at our website. I told the people that "I had seen the Big Dipper changing form, specifically in the handle of the dipper." Here are some excerpts from that article and radio broadcast.

"Over the last few months, at various meetings across the Northwest, I have been telling you that various formations of the cosmos and galaxies are going to be altered—alterations that no one ever dreamed possible. I have also shared how the Lord showed me that the maps of astronomy would be rewritten and redesigned in light of an enormous shift and new discoveries in the heavens above. He has directed me to prophetically declare, time after time, about unusual wonders that would take place in the skies above and the outer limits of space. At these meetings I gave an example of what one of those changes would be. I described how the Lord had shown me that the formations of the stars would change.

"One of my examples was that the *Big Dipper* and the *Little Dipper* would in some way be altered. I gave specific details about the handle of the Big Dipper somehow changing. I added that I did not have the exact knowledge of how the dipper would change, just that it would."

The following text is an excerpt from an article entitled "A Brilliant Hour" from Space.com on **December 9, 2009.**

New Star Found In Big Dipper
One of the stars that make the bend in the ladle's handle, Alcor, has a smaller red dwarf companion, new observations have revealed.

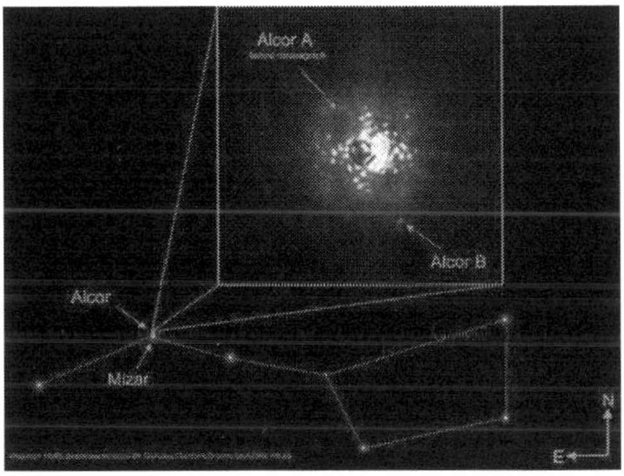

In the article that I wrote, I had to add my thoughts:

"Wow! I have to say it again, 'God is so amazing!' I've never had so much fun! The handle of the Big Dipper has been altered! It has another star! Now it's a glorious dipper of another kind! Come on! You've got to love it! For thousands of years this particular star formation has been seen as unchanged, until now, and the best part is, it is only the beginning. I was reminded of the early episodes of Superman. Part of the intro to the show went like this, 'Look! Up in the sky! It's a bird! No, it's plane! No, it's Superman!'

"Point being, what appeared to be one thing, after closer examination, turned out to be quite another. As I have mentioned in earlier writings, the wonders and alterations of the entire universe are a sign of heaven merging into the earth. At first, all of the activity in the cosmos will look like one thing, but soon it will become something quite different, something very supernatural."

"In Acts 2:19, the word 'wonders' comes from the Greek word '*teras*,' which means prodigy or omen. An omen is defined as 'a phenomenon that is believed to foretell the future, often signifying the advent of change.' This particular omen is in reference to something very good, something very powerful and glorious. In fact the entire earth is about to witness some amazing omens in the heavens above that will cause millions to tremble at the awesome glory and power of God. Right now, the history of the outer limits is being rewritten. If I can stretch you even a little further, there are changes taking place in the third heaven as well. We just assume because something is eternal it is unchanging. Oh, are we in for a surprise."

I ended the article with this final paragraph:

"The beginning movement of this galactic activity is simply God getting the people in the earth to look up. Then suddenly, a divine eruption will occur. A sudden display of light, color and sounds unlike anything we have ever witnessed before since the time of creation. The theory of the 'Big Bang' is coming to a screeching halt. We are living in a time when the lies of creation are going to be exposed for what they really are: foolish deception."

SUPERNATURAL ACTIVATION

Some are inclined to think that most of the activity above the heavens requires little assistance, if any, from the activity on earth. I disagree. As I mentioned earlier, the spiritual activity on earth has a direct impact on all of creation, including the heavens above. I'm not implying that we're the ones who keep the sun and moon shining and the stars suspended in space. The spoken word of God in the beginning is the same force that holds the heavens in place today. However, since the beginning of time, God has always called upon our participation. Our participation with God, in God, has always been an expected part of our inheritance. We are all called to be co-creators with Him. If I may, I would like to expound a bit further on Acts 2.

"Even on My bond slaves, both men and women, I will in those days pour forth of My Spirit and they shall prophesy, and I will grant wonders in the sky above and signs on the earth below..." (Acts 2:18-19)

My summary of these portions of scripture is, "through prophecy, God will show wonders in the sky or heaven above and signs in the earth below." The words *sky* and *heaven* have the same basic meaning, whether in Greek or Hebrew, implying all the layers above: sky, space, and celestial realms. Through prophecy, we are given access to all the above. Through prophecy, we are able to activate the supernatural on earth and in heaven above. When God spoke to Ezekiel saying, **"Can these bones live!?",** He wasn't just asking Ezekiel a question; He was calling him to action. God was telling Ezekiel that, if you believe these bones can live, then prophesy to these bones! **(Ezekiel 37:3-10).**

When Joshua marched around the walls of Jericho, he expected them to come down. When he commanded the sun to be still, he expected it to obey his command. Come on! Who thinks like that?

That's the kind of mind I want. That's the kind of faith I want to live in. There's no doubt that the influence of Moses in Joshua's life left a profound impact on him. Imagine Joshua watching God perform His will through the life of Moses. Year after year, through this humble servant, Joshua was being conditioned to carry the torch of heaven into the future.

I was not so fortunate as to have a spiritual mentor in my life like Joshua. Some of the greatest spiritual influences in my life have come from afar. Men and women who never knew me personally have had a tremendous impact on my future. I am extremely grateful for their contribution to my life. Because of their commitment to advancing the kingdom of God, I have become extremely motivated to prophesy with great faith and certainty. I know my words can inspire action and initiate the movement of heaven on earth and in the heavens above.

This is no different than someone who has great faith in praying for the sick. They expect the people for whom they are praying to be healed. They are confident that God will perform His word. They are expecting it to happen and are surprised when it doesn't. This is the kind of faith God is continually building in me, the kind He wants to build in all of us. While some are scratching their heads, wondering if it's true, I'm immediately looking for the fruit of it. Every time something outrageous comes to pass, my faith increases immensely. I am extremely motivated to walk in this realm of faith and encourage others to do the same.

For the past 15+ years, I have been living in a cave. Although that cave will always be my secret place, I know it's time to come out. I pray you hear this correctly; all of creation has been waiting for me to come out and perform great exploits. So here I am. I am a responder, an activator of the knowledge of the Spirit. You need to know this: All of creation is waiting for you.

It's time to come out into the open and do what you were born to do. This is your future. This is the future for whosoever will dare to be bold and move out in faith and reveal the power and glory of God's kingdom on earth. Whether you are a farmer or a banker, these characteristics are destined to become a part of your life to some degree.

When future storms arise and catastrophic events try to destroy men, women, and children, I want to be there, in the Spirit, ready to head them off at the pass. I want to stand there and say, "Wind, be still!

Sun, stand still! Rain, come! Mountain, be moved!"

COMET HOLMES

I believe this next prophetic word didn't just predict future movement, but created it. I remember very well the intense unction of the Spirit that was on me that day and the sudden burst of light that appeared above me, as if I were suspended in space, echoing the word of the Lord across the galaxy. These are the words I prophesied at a Mountain Top gathering on **October 24, 2007, at approximately 6:45 AM:**

"There is a glory that is much greater, says the Spirit of the Lord, one that breaks the barrier of light. One that breaks the barrier of light, and so there shall be. A great display! A barrier of light shall be broken, says the Spirit of the Lord, a light that will illuminate into areas of the planet that you have never seen before."

"An increasing light that will shine forth. Something that was dark, they could not see, they will begin to see, says the Spirit of the Lord. For there is a light that will shine, even in space. A place that was dark and they said, 'there is nothing there.' Yeah, there is something there. It just lacked the light to see what they needed to see. I can hear the Spirit say even now, 'Watch! Watch! As the light begins to shine. And this will be a sign that the light shines in the darkness! The light shines in the darkness! The light shines in the darkness! And what you thought was dead will come to life,' says the Spirit of the Lord!"

On that same day (October 24, 2007) **at 1:41 PM Eastern time**, Space.com reported that an unusual light had suddenly appeared in space. Given the three-hour time difference from Pacific time to Eastern time, the event occurred roughly three to four hours after the prophecy. Also bear in mind that this cosmos event did not hit the mainstream media until 24 to 48 hours later. Only then was it affirmed that it was Comet Holmes that had suddenly been illuminated, becoming 400,000 times brighter.

Reports came in from all over the world of people seeing this extraordinary phenomenon. An Iranian astronomer in Tehran, Babak Tafreshi, reported being able to see this huge light in space with his naked eye. Here are few of those reports:

NewScientist

Comet brightens mysteriously by a factor of a million

By Maggie McKee

22:04 25 October 2007

Dramatic Comet Outburst Could Last Weeks

By Robert Roy Britt

Senior Science Writer

posted: 26 October 2007 02:09 pm ET

"Comet Holmes had in recent years only been visible through telescopes until a dramatic outburst made it visible to the naked eye. In fewer than 24 hours, it brightened by a factor of nearly 400,000. It has now brightened by a factor of a million times of what it was before the outburst, a change "absolutely unprecedented in the annals of commentary astronomy," said Joe Rao, SPACE.com's Skywatching Columnist."

I know what many of you are thinking right now. Do I really think I had something to do with this sudden burst of light appearing in space? Absolutely. I believe the unction of the Spirit on my words in that moment caused Comet Holmes to respond to the word of the Lord. I wasn't just predicting a future action in the cosmos, I was creating movement in the outer limits of space. I was aligning myself with the intentions of my Father. I was exercising my eternal inheritance as a co-creator with God. Yes! It is true! Thank you, Jesus, for affording us, your people, the opportunity to live supernaturally on earth. Do I think I was the only one? No, I don't. I believe that, if the truth were fully known, others in the world were receiving the revelation of that divine moment in the spirit and acting on it accordingly.

Comet Holmes was discovered by an astronomer named Edwin Holmes on November 6, 1892. There's an interesting correlation between the action of the comet then and now. In 1892, this same comet suddenly became illuminated—not nearly as bright then as now, but bright enough for Edwin Holmes to discover its existence. Now, here we are again, more than a hundred years later, and Comet Holmes catches the eyes of the world again through its unusual brightness. You see where I'm going with this? It was the brightness of its existence that caused the world to take notice—then and now. This is the meaning behind this particular prophetic word.

The hour of illumination is upon us. What the world could not see before, they will see now. The brightness of God's glory will come upon His people suddenly. The people of God have broken through a barrier of light that is intended to illuminate the kingdom of God on earth a million times over. The body of Christ is postured to suddenly burst into view. The glory of the Lord will be visibly displayed before the entire world. Yes! Come on! We're kicking it God! Let it be so even now!

A CELESTIAL ECLIPSE

In keeping with the article "A Brilliant Hour," I wrote another piece that read:

"See the sun shine! See the sun shine! See the sun and the moon, for a great wonder will appear there! See the sun shine! See the sun shine! For right now, in this time, I will give you a sign, a sign in the sun and the moon!"

The same article included the following paragraph:

"We are living in a time when *unusual attention will be given to the sun and the moon, as well as unusual activity that will occur because of their light and movement.* This unusual observance will be the result of a wonder from heaven indicating

that we have entered into a time of extraordinary brilliance. We are about to witness some phenomenal displays of God's brilliant glory, both in the heavens and in the earth."

On **January 15, 2010**, a solar eclipse occurred, lasting 11 minutes and 8 seconds. Now mind you, as I have mentioned in previous writings, I had always been naïve when it came to the obvious movements of our solar system. Although I am far more knowledgeable now than before, I didn't know then that NASA could tell you when an eclipse was scheduled to occur ten years in advance. I also didn't know that scientists could give you an accurate timeframe of how long an eclipse would last. Knowing that this information can easily be found online now takes away a piece of the prophetic edge that it could have otherwise had.

Nonetheless, this recent historical event was reported by Khaleej Times ONLINE as a "Celestial event etched in minds of enthusiasts."

redOrbit reported:

THE LONGEST ECLIPSE FOR 1000 YEARS SEEN OVER AFRICA AND ASIA.

It was also noted as being the longest annular eclipse of the third millennium:

"NASA says that its path will then lead across the Indian Ocean, where the duration of "annularity" will be 11 minutes and eight seconds. This will make it "the longest annular eclipse of the 3rd Millennium. This record will not be beaten until December 23, 3043.

Once again, I wrote:

"There is an unusual alignment, unusual activity, occurring in the heavens, in space, and in the earth. This heavenly movement is the result of the glory of God bringing His people into the brilliance of His love. The purity of heaven has risen in the hearts of God's people, so much so, that what was once termed as 'unapproachable light' (1Timothy 6:16) is now becoming very approachable. The evidence of this pure presence

is causing the entire universe to respond in a glorious manner; thus an unusual alignment is rapidly developing. We have entered into another realm of light; of kingdom revelation. We have been clothed with another layer of glory."

It's important to recognize that this kind of movement marks the beginning of an unusual alignment occurring in the spiritual government of God's kingdom on earth, which will obviously have a huge impact on the natural government of this nation and the world. Men and women of God are beginning to align themselves with one another in a unique fashion as the spirit of the Lord leads them.

SEE THE SUN SHINE

Let's not forget the prophetic portion about the sun. According to the word of the Lord, the sun will also play out a prophetic role in capturing the attention of the entire world. The Lord said,

"See the sun shine! See the sun shine! See the sun and the moon for a great wonder will appear there! See the sun shine!"

For those of you who have been following the latest reports about the action in space, I'm sure you've heard about the unusual display of solar flares erupting at an enormous rate and intensity. It used to be that the sun would flare up within the parameters of prediction. However, in 2010, the sun has proven to be anything but predictable.

On June 11, 2010, **Science News** released the

following report:

"Although the sun has been rather predictable during the past 50 or 60 years, it recently has become less predictable, Kintner said, noting such activity calls into question man's understanding of how the sun operates and the ability to predict its impact on technology." (ScienceNews.com)

The next week, on July 19, 2010, **Space.com** announced that, "Solar flare activity continues to increase."

When you study some of the basic activity occurring around the sun, you quickly discover that the sun generates its own atmosphere. It's believed that the twists in the sun's magnetic field create massive flares that erupt from the sun's surface. When these eruptions occur, they can release over a billion mega tons of TNT. A single flare from the sun can dispense millions of particles toward the earth's atmosphere. When these particles make contact with the magnetic field shielding the earth, they disperse around the field toward the polar regions of the earth, resulting in a beautiful display of color in the night sky known as the northern and southern lights, or auroras.

With respect to the word of the Lord and this

enormous display of power, the sun's current activity is emanating a violent spiritual force that is currently increasing on earth. This unusual display of power is being propelled by a violent thirst and hunger for the things of God. Like the flares of the sun, the people of God are about to burst into a beautiful display of glory. We are on the verge of shining brighter than anyone ever imagined. Contrary to the foolishness of Hollywood and the scientific belief that we are inching closer to final devastation, we have in fact entered into one of the most glorious realms of all time. These are not the final voyages of the sons of God in the earth; these are a mere prelude of what no eye or ear has ever seen or heard before.

GLOBAL SHIFT

On **September 6, 2009,** at Mountain Top International in Yakima, Washington, this portion of prophesy came forth during a time of prayer and worship.

Quote:

"Come on! Come on! The rotation of the earth is beginning to shift; it's shifting on its axis right now. There's a movement that is taking place in the cosmos. What is this unusual movement, this unusual alignment that is taking place? It's an alignment that is not yet visible in space. What is this unusual alignment that is occurring right now? This alignment will appear and they will say, 'what is this alignment in space?' The stars and planets are lining up. Why? Because

there's an unusual alignment on the earth, an unusual alignment in the kingdom of your God. People lining up with Me, says the Lord. They are getting in sync with Me. They are coming into timing with Me. There's an unusual alignment in the earth. Come on! Declare now! It is sealed! It is sealed."

During this time of worship, I remember feeling the earth shift with such intensity that I lost balance and almost fell off the stool I was sitting on, with guitar in hand. Immediately following this word, I stood in front of the people and told them what I had seen in the Spirit. I formed my hands in the shape of a globe and said, "I saw the earth rotating and then suddenly shifting on its axis." I went on to describe how this shift appeared to be instigated by a sudden movement or jolt in the earth.

A few months later, on **February 27, 2010,** Chile experienced an earthquake. This Chilean earthquake had been preceded by a more devastating earthquake one month prior, shaking the region of Haiti, killing more than 230,000 people. Following the aftermath of the Chilean quake, the national media released the following report.

NATIONAL GEOGRAPHIC

"Chile Earthquake Altered Earth Axis, Shortening Day."

"The earthquake that struck Chile was certainly less deadly than the one that hit Haiti. But the Chilean tremors were so powerful that they have shifted Earth's axis and shortened the days.
According to scientists, any natural occurrence that moves a large amount of Earth's mass from one part to the other leads to changes in planet's rotation."

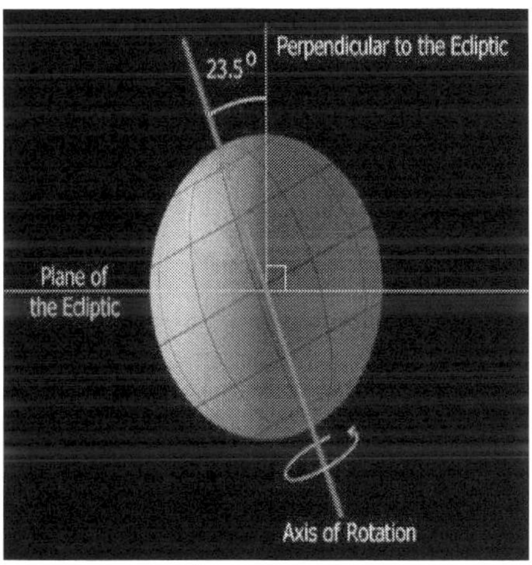

I believe while we were worshiping and prophesying the word of the Lord, a shift occurred in the spiritual realm—a shift so intense that it literally rocked the earth. Of course this seems absurd. Such actions always seem so. Yet, biblical history has recorded the practice of such instances more incongruous than this. Several examples are included in the Old and New Testaments, where the shaking of the earth was the direct result of the action of God's people. When Jonathan and his armor bearer overtook a garrison of Philistines, the earth literally trembled beneath their feet because of the might of the Lord that was upon them.

"That first slaughter which Jonathan and his armor bearer made was about twenty men within about half a furrow in an acre of land, And there was a trembling in the camp, in the field, and among all the people. Even the garrison and the raiders trembled, and the earth quaked so that it became a great trembling." (1Sam14:1415)

Job responded to his critics, saying,

"Speak to the earth, and let it teach you; And let the fish of the sea declare to you." (Job 12:8)

How do you learn from the earth and fish of the sea by speaking to it? The Hebrew word for *speak* is "siyach." It has several meanings, but in respect to this text it means to study, sing, speak, or even declare. If you study the earth, it will teach you the attributes of God. If you speak to it; declare the word of the Lord to it, its response to the word from you will reveal the power of God in you. If you sing to the creatures of the sea like David did to the earth, they will show you just how glorious your words truly are.

Paul and Silas knew firsthand how powerful praise and worship really were.

"But about midnight Paul and Silas were praying and singing hymns of praise to God, and the prisoners were listening to them; and suddenly there came a great earthquake, so that the foundations of the prison house were shaken; and immediately all the doors were opened and everyone's chains were unfastened." (Acts 16:25-27)

They knew what it was like to sing unto the Lord at the midnight hour of their lives. Imagine their surprise when—in the middle of some intense worship—the earth began to shake and the shackles fell from their feet. Shaking the foundation of the prison meant the shockwaves of the earthquake took the doors right off their hinges. Ha! You've got to love it. Let me just add some prophetic insight here.

"In what seems to be the last hour in this nation, the earth will shake, and those who have been in bondage to the works of the enemy will be freed."

Now back to the subject at hand. I would be doing you a disservice if I failed to point out the intentions of God behind this amazing phenomenon of tilting the earth. The first portion of this prophetic declaration signified "**a shift or movement that would lead to an unusual alignment.**" Over the last couple of years, there has been much discussion across the world concerning "the shift." I believe the tilting of the earth exemplifies a change so great that the very idea of such a change seems entirely impossible.

This is the season in which you can expect your position in God and in the world to dramatically change. God is giving you access into regions of the world you never dreamed possible. The obstacles in your life that have appeared immovable are going to move out of your way. Realms of the Spirit that you have been leaning into are suddenly going to be opened to you. The government of this nation that appears to have crossed beyond the line of no return is suddenly going to tilt into a brand new direction—not for the worse, but for the better. Yes it will appear for the worse, but only momentarily.

Please hear what I am saying. Most believed it was impossible for the earth to change its rotation, but it did. Most never thought they would live to see the day when the angle of the planet would be anything different than what it has always been, but they have. This season is not about what we thought would be possible, but what is impossible.

UNUSUAL ALIGNMENT

Of course we can't forget the finale of this same prophetic utterance:

"What is this unusual movement, this unusual alignment that is taking place? It's an alignment that is not yet visible in space. What is this unusual alignment that is occurring right now? This alignment will appear and they will say, 'what is this alignment in space?' The stars and planets are lining up. Why? Because there is an unusual alignment in the earth. An unusual alignment in the kingdom of your God. People lining up with Me, says the Lord. They are getting in sync with Me. They are coming into timing with Me. There's an unusual alignment in the earth."

The Lord told us that there was an unusual alignment about to take place with the stars and planets in space. He said that this alignment wasn't visible, meaning that it would occur at some point in the future. The first part of this word was the tilting of the earth while the second part points to the unique aligning of the stars and planets.

A short time later, after this word came forth, the Hollywood movie about 2012 was brought to my attention. Evidently it had something to do with sun flares and an unusual lining of the planets. However, let me assure you, the alignment to which God is referring is not one of those. This future aligning in the cosmos has everything to do with a wonderful display of the glory of God beyond anything we have ever witnessed before. This unique galactic expression is directly related to a special uniting of the people of God on earth. It's a portrayal of a beautiful harmony in the kingdom of God never before demonstrated on earth. Each kingdom in this world will in some way yield a significant measure of its influence to the kingdom of God over the course of the next ten years. This willingness to surrender to the pleasures of heaven will be prompted by a powerful display of the love, glory, and power of God in ways never witnessed before by this generation.

Time and time again I have seen a wonderful display amongst the stars above, reflecting color and light in ways that are far beyond the reason of any scientific understanding. The galaxies above are preparing for one of the greatest light shows the world has ever seen. Just as the people celebrated the entry of Jesus into the city of Jerusalem, so will many tribes and nations celebrate His glorious appearance once again. In conjunction with all tribes and nations, all of creation is adorning itself with astounding movements, sounds, and colors. The heavens will dance like we have never seen them dance before. They will align themselves with the sound of heaven within us. Let me encourage you to set your mind on things above and not on things below, for our Redeemer lives and the entire world shall know it.

SURPRISE FIREBALL

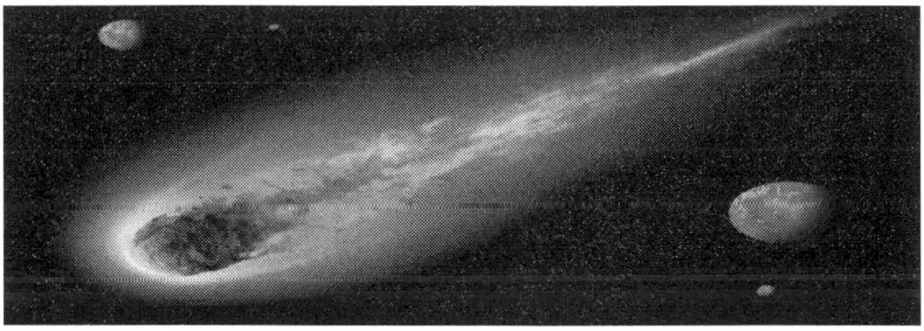

On **November 15, 2009,** during a prophetic gathering at the Healing Rooms event center in Spokane, Washington, I prophesied this word:

"Hear the word of the Lord, 'In just a few **days I'm going to catch you by surprise, look to the heavens; look to the skies! In just a** few **days I'm going to catch you by surprise, look to the heavens; look to the skies! This is a time for unusual displays, for signs and wonders to appear in the heavens, the skies, and space. In just a few days I'm going to catch you by surprise, so look to the heavens look to the skies!' I can hear the Lord say, "Happy Birthday to you! Happy Birthday to you! Happy Birthday to you!"**

A few days later, on **November 18, 2009**, national news networks reported the following:

NBC – A stunning sight lit up the sky over Utah and several western states Wednesday.

SpaceWeather.com sent out this report:

GREAT WESTERN FIREBALL: Yesterday, Nov. 18th, something exploded in the atmosphere above the western United States. Witnesses in Colorado, Utah, Wyoming and Idaho say the fireball "turned night into day" and issued shock waves that "shook the ground" when it exploded just after midnight Mountain Standard Time. The fireball was so bright it actually turned the sky noontime blue, as shown in this image from KSL TV in Utah.

Approximately 6 hours after the fireball, people in Utah and Colorado got another surprise. As the sun rose over those states, a twisting electric-blue cloud appeared in the dawn sky:

“These curious clouds on the horizon caught my attention just before sunrise," says photographer Don Brown of Park City , Utah. "They were strangely bright relative to the rest of the sky."

“The cloud strongly resembles artificial noctilucent clouds formed at high altitudes by rocket and shuttle launches. Yet there was no (officially reported) rocket launch at dawn on Nov. 18th. Could the cloud be associated with the fireball? The geographical coincidence is certainly striking. Debris from the fireball should have dissipated by sunrise, but the cloud remains unexplained and a connection to the fireball cannot yet be dismissed.”

It seemed a bit odd to me when we started singing "Happy Birthday." Such oddity is often a part of our journey in prophetic worship. However, I later discovered this surprise manifestation in the heavens landed on the eve of Jim Leuschan's birthday.

Jim is the apostolic oversight of the Sunday Healing Rooms church services in Spokane. Everyone knew that we had entered into an unprecedented moment in history—a historical time when spectacular displays are going to reveal themselves in a manner the world has never seen before. This was yet another sign of a sudden eruption from heaven appearing on earth. The world is going to be surprised, awed, and shocked by signs and wonders appearing on earth and above it.

I know this sounds a bit repetitious, but I have to say it, again and again: Prepare yourself for spectacular events on and above the earth.

When I heard the Lord singing "Happy Birthday," I believe His intentions were twofold. The fact that this event landed on the eve of Jim's birthday is a revelation of countless men and women who are about to be birthed into another realm of spiritual understanding and supernatural activity. It is also the birthing of a new era in the Spirit where the entire universe responds to the supernatural forces of heaven. I know I am echoing previous chapters, but there's no way around it, so let's delve into God's intentions behind this surprise encounter.

First, when this fireball broke the atmosphere, many astrologers were positioned to witness a Leonid event. They were surprised by something far more profound. This is God's way of saying,

"The event you have been preparing for will be interrupted by something much greater."

Second, it was also noted that the entry of this fireball created a sound so loud that it shook the entire Pacific Northwest and then some. This is an indication of an enormous sound barrier that is being broken in the spirit—a sound from heaven that will shake the earth so violently that millions of people will suddenly look toward heaven.

Third, the media also revealed that the light was so intense it turned night into day. It goes without saying that the glory of God is accumulating on earth with such intensity that the darkest regions of the heart and mind are about to be flooded with the light of the gospel of the glory of Jesus Christ. Come on, God!

Finally, the news rooms announced that the aftermath of this event left the skies filled with silvery swirling clouds that lasted for days. Without a doubt these lingering clouds illustrate the lasting redemptive impact that these signs and wonders from heaven will have on the earth and its people. So prepare yourself for one of the greatest heavenly encounters ever known to man.

HOW TO WALK IT OUT

It just wouldn't seem right if I didn't end this book with some practical disciplines on how to live in this kind of mind. I felt somewhat like a prophetic cheerleader while writing this book. "You can do it, yes you can, come on and prophesy! Go team! Go!" But really, how do you turn all of what you have just read into an actual lifestyle?

Every day I am challenged to prophetically explore my surroundings and move deeper into a greater demonstration of prophetically conveying the heart and mind of God on earth. One of the greatest hurdles I had to overcome early on was the willingness to take a risk. I heard a well-known prophet once say, "There are caretakers, risk takers and undertakers; you have to decide which one you will be." You can't venture into the unknown without the willingness to step out of the boat. Risk is part of the prophetic journey, not to mention the courage and boldness to follow the voice of the Lord.

Of course you know you have to pray, spend time with the Lord, and learn His sound, His voice, and His ways. This pertains to anything we do in this life. I find one of the major roadblocks to predicting and creating the future lies within the realm of imagination. You literally have to set your mind on things above. You have to see yourself speaking to creation, commanding it to line up with the intentions of God on earth. This means you have to spend some personal time practicing speaking to the wind, the rain, the sun, and the moon and stars. Just the other day Lori and I were driving down the road when we looked toward the west and saw a huge dark cloud of rain coming our way. We were busy doing some outside work in town and needed some extra clear skies to finish the task at hand. So we simply looked at the impossible and began to command the rainy storm to head in a different direction. Sometime later we looked up and realized the rain had changed its course. I must admit I felt a little goofy commanding the rain to go another direction just so we could finish our chores. I mean who does something like that? Yet, this is what it takes to see the earth respond to the voice of the

Lord. Yes, we could have stopped to consider all the reasons for not acting in such a manner, but the fact is we needed more time to do our work. We could have dismissed the outcome as a mere coincidence, but we didn't. We could've said, "Well, this area needs more rain and that is far more important than what we are doing." After a brief evaluation we decided that was not the case and took charge of the situation. God cares about the simple things going on in our daily lives. Sound crazy? Of course it's crazy. It's supposed to be crazy. You have to be willing to be crazy—in a good way—to do something like this. Never let the times that don't seem to work keep you from stepping out again and again. It's the only way you will ever break the barrier of doubt and unbelief. If you feel like you don't have faith for some areas in your life then focus on the areas you do have faith for. Work your way toward the areas that seem impossible to walk in. A while back I came upon a woodpecker pecking at a huge tree. As I watched, its efforts didn't appear to be making in any difference at all. A few days later, this same woodpecker caught my attention again. I was shocked at the progress this little bird had madc. It had pecked a whole so large that it was able to stick most of its head into it. I thought, "What a perfect example of persistent faith." No matter how impossible the situation may appear at first, stay at it, and you will eventually see the results of your faith at work. Meditating on scriptures is another basic, but powerful tool for enhancing your spiritual senses. Go through the scriptures and study all the other crazies for God who spoke to the winds, sun, and rain. Discover their secrets, and you will discover the keys that unlocked amazing doors of faith and kingdom authority.

You don't entertain this kind of supernatural world just by thinking about it in your spare time. You have to think about it, day in and day out. Find out how this kind of mind fits into your current vocation. Envision yourself as a child of God who has been given unlimited access to explore the universe. When I am going about my daily routine or worshiping the Lord, I envision myself literally dancing among the stars, running moon dust through my hands, passing through clouds full of rain, or watching creatures fly around the throne of God.

Smith Wigglesworth once said, "Preach faith because you want it, and then preach it because you have it." This really is true: Use it or lose it. Practice, practice, practice! Exercise your spiritual senses. Much of my training has come from dwelling in the secret place of the Most High. Like any other gift, the best place to grow is in the fields of life. Wherever the people are the Lord is there also.

I look at all my previous prophetic experiences and realize I have only just begun to walk in the mind and heart of God the way I long to. So, while you are on your journey, exploring the heavens above, just remember, "You can boldly go where no one has ever gone before. The outer limits are yours for the taking." Come on, God! As each day passes, I am highly motivated, even more, to see the invisible realm become visible.

Product Information

If you have enjoyed reading this book you will also enjoy Michael's previous books:

"Beyond Knowledge of Good and Evil" and "Evolution of Another Kind."

Michael's books and teachings can be purchased on line at www.mticenter.com.

You can also log on to the website and sign up for Michael's monthly prophetic articles and future prophecies.

He has written some great articles over the years, some of which were inserted into this book. He has also written articles about future events in the United States and across the world, as well as, other unusual occurrences in the earth.

Watch for Michael's up and coming books in 2010-2011

The Eyes of Luchnos/ A great adventure about a blind woman named Luc, a divine Seer, who takes a young boy (Hajile) on an unforgettable journey, which gives birth to the "Seer's Institute" in the city of Yakima, Washington.

God's Positive and Negative Equation... This is definitely a paradigm shift concerning good and evil. It reveals how every action, everything created and made, is governed by a positive and negative force or energy. Did I just say, "Energy?" Oh yeah! ☺

Left/Right Brain Worship... This revelation explains the concept of "spontaneous worship" in a way few have ever heard before. It will revolutionize your understanding about how the knowledge of God is introduced through the sound of music. It also expounds on some amazing future musical expressions that you can expect to hear in the future.

The Intended Government of God... what a simple, but profound understanding of God's intended government for His people. What is the expected government of this nation destined to look like over the next ten years? What kind of President will we have? What will the White House of this nation look like?

If you are interested in having Michael come to your city you can call 509-457-6584, or write PO Box 43 Yakima, WA 98907...or you can email us at michael@mticenter.com

19123016R00063

Made in the USA
Charleston, SC
07 May 2013